# BOURNEMOUTH AIRPORT
## THROUGH TIME
Mike Phipp

AMBERLEY

First published 2017

Amberley Publishing
The Hill, Stroud, Gloucestershire, GL5 4EP
www.amberley-books.com

Copyright © Mike Phipp, 2017

The right of Mike Phipp to be identified as the
Author of this work has been asserted in accordance with
the Copyrights, Designs and Patents Act 1988.

ISBN  978 1 4456 0552 4 (print)
ISBN  978 1 4456 7398 1 (ebook)

British Library Cataloguing in Publication Data.
A catalogue record for this book is available from the
British Library.

Origination by Amberley Publishing.
Printed in Great Britain.

# Introduction

## False Start

Bournemouth's original airport was established in the 1930s in the nearby town of Christchurch. The grass airfield already in existence there was upgraded at the beginning of 1935 by the newly formed Bournemouth Airport Ltd. Scheduled services by a number of small airlines commenced that summer, serving destinations such as Bristol, Cardiff, Croydon, Guernsey, Plymouth and Ryde. They used four-seater de Havilland Fox Moths and eight-seater de Havilland Dragons, but the services did not prosper as hoped. This was partially due to the restricted size of the airport, with all services ceasing on the outbreak of the Second World War in September 1939.

## RAF Hurn

When the Germans overran Holland, Belgium and northern France, they had many more bases from which to attack Great Britain. The main fear was the probable seaborne invasion of Britain in the early summer of 1940. For this the Luftwaffe would be able to provide cover from its new fighter bases around the Cherbourg Peninsula and it was from these airfields that the Luftwaffe operated during the Battle of Britain. To counter the threat the RAF urgently required new bases along the South Coast – one of these was RAF Hurn.

Various sites to the north of Bournemouth had been surveyed by Sir Alan Cobham in 1938 as part of the plan to replace the airport at Christchurch, so the Air Ministry were able to refer to his reports, with land at Hurn village being requisitioned from the local landowner. Construction commenced in 1940 with three tarmac runways provided, as well as the necessary hardstandings and buildings. Officially opened on 1 August 1941, RAF Hurn was too late to play any part in the Battle of Britain. The first occupant was the Telecommunications Flying Unit, which undertook the development of radar in aircraft. This involved airborne radar to seek out other aircraft and radar in bombers to establish their position over the ground. The Unit departed in May 1942 and was replaced the following month by Armstrong Whitworth Whitleys of No. 38 Wing, Army Co-Operation Command. They were used for training paratroops and towing assault gliders. Many exercises were undertaken, usually over Salisbury Plain, often resulting in Horsa gliders ending up in fields where they shouldn't have been. During the autumn and winter of 1942 the Whitleys undertook leaflet and Special Operations Executive (SOE) supply drops over France. The outdated Whitleys began to be replaced by Albemarles from January 1943 – Hurn being the first airfield to see the type's operational use. Large numbers of Horsas appeared from the spring of 1943, destined for Operation Beggar – the invasion of Sicily from North Africa. The quickest way to get them there was to tow them all the way and Handley Page Halifax tugs from nearby Holmsley South commenced the long journey on 1 June. The local Albemarles also flew to North Africa, from where they towed the Horsas during the successful invasion. Hurn also proved an important airfield for returning Allied aircraft. Many fighters called to refuel before returning to their home bases. It was also used by bombers a long way from home, often arriving with flak damage after long flights over France and Germany. By the end of the year there were three Albemarle squadrons based at Hurn tasked with training exercises with Horsa gliders. This was all part of the build up to D-Day the following summer. However, there were changes at Hurn prior to this.

In March 1944 the Albemarles and Horsas moved out, with the airfield passing to Fighter Command as part of the RAF's 2nd Tactical Air Force. The first arrivals were three RCAF squadrons equipped with Hawker Typhoon fighter-bombers, forming No. 143 Wing. These fighters were modified to carry 1,000 lb bombs under their wings – hence the nickname 'Bombphoons'. They were followed in April by a further three squadrons forming No. 124 Wing, their Typhoons being fitted with rocket projectiles under their wings. The Wings' task was to attack enemy targets in northern France plus enemy shipping encountered in the English Channel. This required a large amount of low-level flying, which was not without danger. During May, attacks were made on German radar sites in Normandy and the Channel Islands. The Typhoons were joined by two de Havilland Mosquito night fighter squadrons, which were able to provide cover on the eve of the D-Day landings. The arrival of D-Day, 6 June, saw over a hundred fighters based at Hurn. No. 143 Wing was first into action, arriving over the beach-head just as the first landing craft were disgorging their troops. No. 124 Wing followed up and many sorties were undertaken over the following hectic days. With long hours of daylight, operations could begin at 3.00 a.m. and continue until 11.30 p.m. Emergency Landing Strips were soon brought into use in Normandy, enabling Allied fighters to land to refuel and re-arm. However, they proved very dusty, resulting in the Hurn-based Typhoons having to return home each evening for the replacement of their engines. The Sabre engines were complicated to maintain and it was quicker to replace the engine than to try and fix the defects. By the end of June both Wings were able to move base permanently to more substantial airfields in northern France. Other Typhoon squadrons passed through Hurn en route to Normandy. In fact, out of twenty Typhoon squadrons operational at the time, fifteen passed through Hurn. There were still some Mosquito operations for a while, including assisting the USAAF. However the Mosquitoes had gone by the end of June, resulting in Hurn being devoid of RAF aircraft.

Hurn was then to be used by the USAAF. In fact, they had used Hurn in the autumn of 1942 as a base for aircraft transporting troops to North Africa to take part in Operation Torch. This had involved large numbers of Douglas C-47 transports, backed up by B-17 Fortress and B-24 Liberator bombers hastily converted as transports. The aircraft first flew to Gibraltar before continuing to North Africa. Among the VIPs to pass through Hurn were Ike Eisenhower and Jimmy Doolittle. The end of June 1944 saw the arrival of six P-61 Black Widow night fighters for comparison trials with the local RAF Mosquitoes. As well as affiliation trials, the P-61s accompanied the Mosquitoes on some operational sorties. The Americans had been concerned as to whether the P-61 was up to the job but their worries were soon dispelled as they outperformed the experienced Mosquito crews. Following the departure of the Mosquitoes, Hurn became USAAF Station 492 for the next few weeks. This saw the arrival of B-26 Marauders of the 397th Bomb Group at the beginning of August. Comprised of four squadrons, the Group's task was to carry out interdiction bombing sorties over northern France to hinder any German resupply attempts. Such was the Allies' progress through France that the Group was able to set up base near Caen by the end of August. RAF Hurn fell almost silent, its part in the Second World War having been completed.

## Initial Airline Operations

BOAC commenced services from Hurn as early as January 1942. Despite it being wartime, the airline already operated limited services from its base at Bristol. RAF Hurn was used as an additional base as it was close to BOAC's existing flying boat base at Poole and, at the time, it was underused by the RAF. The first route was to Cairo using a couple of converted Consolidated Liberators and a Curtiss CW-20 – the twelve-hour flight having to take the long way round via Gibraltar to avoid occupied France. At Cairo there were connections with BOAC's flying boat services to Australia and South Africa. However, the services were not for the public but government ministers and military VIPs who had urgent business overseas. They usually arrived by Pullman train from London Victoria, which also served the flying boat services from Poole. Services expanded at the beginning of 1943 with the arrival of the first of a large number of Douglas Dakotas, as well as additional Liberators. The spring of 1944 saw the first of many Avro Yorks, which gradually took over from the Liberators. The Dakotas, Liberators and Yorks were camouflaged – similar to those in RAF service – but carried civilian registrations and a large Union Jack for identification. The main routes were to Madrid, Lisbon, Cairo and Shannon (for connection to the USA). Over the D-Day period these had to be operated from Bristol or Lyneham, but Hurn's future had already been decided.

In the spring of 1944 the Air Ministry were planning the expansion of the airport for BOAC's future use. At the time there was no suitable airport at London (the existing Croydon and Heston were too small), although

BOAC considered there to be insufficient accommodation at Hurn. Despite this, the airport was transferred from RAF Fighter Command to the Director of Civil Aviation at midnight on 31 October 1944. So, from 1 November, Hurn/Bournemouth became the country's civilian air terminal. New routes saw Dakotas flying to West Africa, with Liberators and Yorks operating to the Far East. As war was still in progress the flights continued to operate via Gibraltar to avoid France. Other airlines to be seen at Bournemouth at the time were KLM, Sabena and ABA Sweden. In November 1944 the wartime censor optimistically described Bournemouth as 'Britain's finest airfield'. For longer distance services, a number of converted Lancaster bombers were ordered for BOAC. Known as Lancastrians, they arrived in the spring of 1945 ready for services to Australia. After proving flights, the service to Sydney commenced on 31 May, the main aim being to carry Royal Mail to India and Australia – initially only nine passengers were carried in the cramped cabin. The service was operated jointly with Qantas, the crews changing at Karachi, with a flight time of 67½ hours. The service was described as serving the needs of the Far Eastern theatre of war. A problem with the former military layout of the airport meant that passenger reception was in Hurn village, some way from the airport. Travel time had to be factored in to ensure the flight got away on time, with BOAC operating seventy-four services a week.

With the return to peace in September 1945, various American airlines made plans to operate transatlantic services to London. The Air Ministry pointed out that there was no airport available at London and that they would have to use Bournemouth alongside BOAC. At the time Heathrow was under construction, but would not be available for some months. Both American Export and Pan American World used Douglas DC-4s to operate proving flights from New York to Bournemouth in September, with the first service by American Export arriving on 24 October. Allowing for two stops, the flight took twenty-four hours. Reports at the time described it as arriving at London (Hurn Airport), England. Early in 1946 both airlines switched to Lockheed Constellations, with flight time reduced to twelve hours. BOAC commenced services to Johannesburg in November 1945, which were operated by Yorks in conjunction with South African Airways. Bournemouth's importance diminished on 31 May 1946 with the opening of London Airport, which resulted in the airlines switching their services the following day. However, there was still plenty of activity at Bournemouth as it remained BOAC's maintenance and servicing base for some years, as there were no hangars yet at London. The airline also used Bournemouth as a base for its Development Flight and for crew training. More importantly, Bournemouth was designated the diversion airport for London – the Air Ministry considered it a satellite to London. In due course hangars were built at London and BOAC moved its maintenance work there in the summer of 1950. The Development Flight undertook trials of a number of new airliners including the de Havilland Dove, Vickers Viking, Handley Page Hermes and the de Havilland Comet – the world's first jet airliner. It was easier to carry out crew training at a relatively quiet Bournemouth than an ever-expanding London. Training continued until 1959, when the Bristol Britannia was in use – BOAC's final propeller airliner. A few Comet 4s were seen in 1958 but, being jets, it was more appropriate to carry out training somewhere more remote. The airport was also used by international airlines for crew training. Airliners from the likes of Pan American, Qantas and Trans-Canada visited from London in between services. During the late 1940s and 1950s, Bournemouth was an important diversion airport, especially when the London area was blanketed by fog. The first major diversion was in November 1946 when BOAC provided staff from Poole to deal with the aircraft. One in November 1948 saw over a hundred airliners diverted, with the bad weather resulting in coaches taking eight hours to get passengers to London. The last major diversion with piston engine airliners was in December 1958. Many of the world's major airlines were to be seen at Bournemouth on such occasions – Air India, El Al, Iberia, KLM, Pan American, Qantas, SAS, Sabena, Swiss Air and TWA.

In the late 1940s there were attempts to establish local air services from Bournemouth. The summer of 1947 saw flights from Croydon to Jersey operated by de Havilland Dragon Rapides and these were repeated the following summers. It wasn't until the summer of 1952 that regular services commenced, operated by Jersey Airlines from the Channel Islands northwards to Manchester. Initially, Dragon Rapides were used, but Herons arrived for the summer 1954 season. A terminal area was made available in the former wartime wooden buildings within the airport, being more convenient than that established in Hurn village. In due course the public found they could also gain access to see the airliners coming and going. A small area was fenced off, provided with tables and chairs so that visitors could have a bun and cup of tea from the adjacent terminal café. Bournemouth was used by a number of airlines to clear customs en route to the Channel Islands as customs facilities still weren't available at many airports. By the spring of 1953 the airport was officially known as Bournemouth (Hurn) Airport, although for many years one of the main notice boards still proclaimed it as Hurn Airport.

There were no light aircraft based at Bournemouth in the 1950s as these were to be found at nearby Christchurch airfield. However, pleasure flights were available in the mid-1950s in a de Havilland Dove or a Miles Aerovan.

## Industry

With the departure of BOAC's maintenance base to London, new occupants were soon found for the vacated hangars. One was taken over by de Havilland as a flight test base for aircraft produced at the former Airspeed factory at Christchurch. During 1952/53 this comprised of Ambassador airliners destined for BEA, followed by a succession of jet fighters. There were Venoms and Sea Venoms for the RAF and Royal Navy, plus a large number of Vampire Trainers – many for export. Sea Vixens for the Royal Navy appeared from 1957, but all testing moved to Hatfield in 1960 on re-organisation within the company.

The main user of BOAC's hangars was Vickers-Armstrongs of Weybridge, who set up a temporary flight test base in the summer of 1951. Prototypes of the Varsity trainer, Viscount airliner and Valiant bomber were to be seen. Vickers realised that they needed extra production capacity and decided to transfer Varsity production from Weybridge to Hurn, with the first one flying in November 1951. Vickers always referred to this as their Hurn site – not Bournemouth. Viscount production got under way at Weybridge and was followed from December 1953 by aircraft from the second production line at Hurn. The Viscount proved so successful that it was sold to the almost impenetrable North American market. Trans-Canada Air Lines placed an initial order in November 1952 and this was followed by the one from Capital Airlines of Washington in June 1954. Viscounts were sold around the world with the Hurn site producing two-thirds of them, the final one being delivered to China in April 1964.

Vickers-Armstrongs became part of the British Aircraft Corporation in July 1960 and one of the early projects was a jet replacement for the Viscount. This led to the BAC One-Eleven, which followed the Viscount down the production line at Hurn, entering service in April 1965. As with the Viscount, as well as the home and European markets, One-Eleven sales were made to the demanding North America market. In January 1978 BAC became part of British Aerospace following the re-organisation of the UK's aircraft industry. Production had slowed but subsequent orders kept the production line open until 1982. This included a number for Romania, which led to the Rombac Deal in June 1978 where production would be undertaken in Bucharest. Political instability meant that production did not proceed smoothly, with only nine aircraft being completed by 1989. At Hurn One-Eleven work tailed off by the early 1980s and a lack of further development led to the site being closed in the summer of 1984.

Airwork was well established in the aviation world, with operations undertaken in many countries. 1952 saw the formation of the Airwork Fleet Requirement Unit to operate 'target' aircraft on behalf of the Royal Navy for exercises in the English Channel. Although a civilian operation, pilots were former service members eking out a few more hours flying fighters. The first of twenty de Havilland Sea Hornets arrived in 1953, soon to be replaced by Hawker Sea Furies. The Unit entered the jet age in 1957 with the arrival of Hawker Sea Hawks, which flew alongside the Sea Furies until they were taken out of service in 1962. Being faster, the Sea Hawks proved more difficult for the human eye to spot as a potential target, so they received an overall gloss black paint scheme to aid identification. The Unit also provided targets to be shot at, these being drogues towed behind Fairey Fireflies in the early days, until the Fireflies were replaced by Gloster Meteors in 1958. The Unit was often dispatched overseas for fleet operations, their aircraft frequently being sent to Gibraltar or Malta. Supermarine Scimitars replaced the Sea Hawks in 1966 but did not prove satisfactory, so Hawker

Hunters arrived in 1969. At the same time, English Electric Canberras took over the target towing duties. As part of naval re-organisation the FRU moved to Yeovilton in October 1972.

Airwork Services moved their headquarters to the airport in the summer of 1959. The company consolidated its overhaul business from a number of other locations, mainly dealing with airliners, and were based in the former de Havilland hangar. This saw a variety of exotic Dakotas, Doves, DC-4s and Vikings over the years. Airwork also had contracts with various Middle Eastern air forces to supply them with aircraft, with many passing through Bournemouth. Examples included Saudi Hunters, Abu Dhabi Caribous, Oman and Singapore Strikemasters, Sudan Jet Provosts and Oman Skyvans. These would be delivered by Airwork's civilian pilots. From December 1978 Airwork also maintained the Bournemouth-based RAF Bulldogs of the Southampton University Air Squadron and Chipmunks of No. 2 Air Experience Flight. Airwork became part of the Bombardier Group in October 1993.

In 1949 the School of Air Traffic Control was established in former RAF huts near the airport's entrance. It trained civilian air controllers and assistants, initially from Britain but later from over a hundred overseas countries. Part of the training involved the students visiting the control tower to guide Radar Target Oxfords and Doves on, hopefully, a successful talk-down approach and landing. The wartime huts were falling apart and so a large, modern building was brought into use in September 1962. The expansion of air travel and the introduction of jet airliners meant that training had to be kept up to date. This saw the ATC Evaluation Unit move into the new premises, being involved in the development of new technologies and procedures. To reflect its importance, the School was renamed the College of ATC in 1968. Computerisation and the introduction of GPS played a great part in the College's teaching in the 1980s, with an increased demand for controllers resulting in an extension being added in 1991. Students received eighteen months' training followed by a further eighteen months being monitored 'on the job'. In 1995 the Evaluation Unit was renamed the Air Traffic Management Development Centre, continuing with research and development work. To keep up with modern developments, the College and the ATMDC needed up-to-date accommodation to house the latest equipment and training aids. This was established at Whiteley, near Fareham, with the move made in August 2011.

Flight Refuelling was well established in the aviation field. In 1985 it formed FR Aviation (now known as Cobham Aviation) at Bournemouth to operate a fleet of Dassault Falcon 20s on behalf of the Royal Navy in a similar manner to the earlier Airwork FRU. Acting as targets, the Falcons carried underwing stores for a variety of roles, such as ECM pods to jam ships' radar and others housing target towing equipment. The Falcons undertook exercises with the Royal Navy in the English Channel, as well as undertaking detachments to the Mediterranean. Over the years the Falcons have become a frequent sight over the area, often returning to the airport in pairs, and will continue their role for a few more years to come. FRA also undertook conversion work on RAF VC10s in the 1990s to convert them to a dual transport/tanker role. It was later involved in the RAF Voyager tanker/transport programme.

European Aviation purchased British Airways' surplus fleet of BAC One-Elevens in May 1993 and ferried them to Bournemouth. Using the former BAC hangars, it established its own Air Charter division to operate some of the fleet, with others chartered to other airlines. In the spring of 1998 European purchased Sabena's Boeing 737 fleet to replace the noisy One-Elevens. Because of noise regulations they were taken out of service in 2002, with European operating a farewell flight from the airport on 31 March. A fleet of ex-British Airways Boeing 747s were later operated for a brief period. European ceased airline operations in November 2008, continuing with its maintenance business.

## Current Operations

Bournemouth-Hurn Airport was run by the Board of Trade until 1 April 1969, when it was sold to Bournemouth and Dorset councils. Until the 1990s scheduled services were mainly shorter routes such as the Channel Islands, Paris, Manchester and Glasgow. Airlines were now names from the past – including BEA, British United, Cambrian, Channel Airways, Dan-Air and Silver City. Inclusive Tours holidays to the

Mediterranean commenced in 1958, with operations by local travel firm Bath Travel. These grew over the years, led by its flamboyant chairman, Peter Bath. Initially aircraft were chartered from a variety of UK and European airlines, but in the spring of 1993 they set up their own airline – Palmair. As well as holiday flights, Palmair undertook day trips to European capitals and these proved very popular over the years. However, there was a change to services from Bournemouth with the arrival of Ryanair in May 1995 offering flights to Dublin for £59.99. At the time no one realised the effect that low-cost carriers were to have on future air travel. Jersey European was the last of the old-style carriers at Bournemouth, ending its services in October 1993. Also flying from Bournemouth was Channel Express, who operated cargo flights to and from the Channel Islands with a fleet of Handley Page Dart-Heralds and Fokker F27s. The company also held the contract to operate the nightly Royal Mail flights northwards to Liverpool, plus early morning newspaper flights to the Channel Islands. Other airlines later operated these services, continuing until the Royal Mail cancelled the contract in November 2015.

Bournemouth's wooden terminal buildings were replaced by a modern terminal, which opened in September 1984, being designed to handle aircraft such as sixty-seat Fokker F27s and HS748s. Over the years there were a number of Government reports concerning expansion of airports in the south, often recommending Bournemouth for development. The two local councils realised they did not have the capital to invest further in the airport, which they sold to the National Express Group in April 1995. Further investment was planned for Bournemouth International Airport, with an extension to the main runway opened in April 1996. This saw a visit of Concorde to officially open the runway extension – 08/26 was now 2,271 metres long and fully Category III equipped. Further Concorde charters from Bournemouth were organised by Bath Travel. National Express also drew up plans for a larger terminal to cope with a million passengers a year. This did not proceed as passenger numbers did not increase as hoped and then the plans were called in by the government as the land fell within Green Belt. In the summer of 2000 National Express decided to pull out of airport operations, with Bournemouth Airport being acquired by the Manchester Airports Group in March 2001; the International part of the name was dropped.

The majority of movements at Bournemouth are training flights of one form or another. Due to rising costs there is less work for the flying clubs, but there is still a demand for commercial pilot training. This mainly sees the likes of Beech Duchesses, Diamond Twin Stars and Piper Senecas on circuits. With simulators now widely used there is little use of an actual airliner for training, as was the case thirty years ago. The RAF and Royal Navy also make almost daily use of the airport for training, with any current service type appearing. For the RAF the most common are Chinooks and Hercules, with Atlas and Globemasters appearing occasionally. From Yeovilton the Navy send Merlins and Wildcats, with QinetiQ at Boscombe Down also providing a selection of their test fleet. Bournemouth is also the destination of Royal Air Force of Oman Airbus A320s and Hercules when visiting the UK.

In recent years the Northern Aviation Business Park has been greatly expanded, and some of the earlier hangars are still in use. European Aviation is based in the former BAC ones for handling Boeing 737 overhauls, with the adjacent hangar used for airliner repainting. There are a large number of business aircraft based here with a variety of operators. The Citation Centre has been here since 1979, handling the current range of Cessna executive jets which are currently in a modern hangar and now known as Signature TechnicAir. Jetworks, JETS and Thurston Aviation also house a range of executive jets. Another hangar houses the PC-12 Service Centre, and Honeywell Aerospace and Meggitt are other well-known names housed within the Park. These businesses all add to aircraft activity at the airport. AIM Aviation has also been at Bournemouth for many years, originally undertaking maintenance work and airliner painting in the 1990s. Recently it has concentrated on aerospace interior furnishings and at the end of 2016 AIM Altitude opened a large new complex to cope with additional work. This was followed by another large unit – this time for Curtiss-Wright Corp. At the present time the Aviation Business Park is being actively developed by Manchester Airports Group, with its 200 businesses providing the majority of Bournemouth Airport's income.

The Bournemouth Aviation Museum was originally established in one of the hangars on the airport in August 1999. Here it had the advantage of housing active historic aircraft. The Museum had to move and it relocated to its present site adjacent to the airport in 2008. It prides itself for being a 'hands on' location for children of all ages, with access to the majority of aircraft and cockpits. These include the fuselage of a former Palmair Boeing 737 and a locally built BAC One-Eleven.

Passenger numbers increased with the arrival in March 2005 of Thomson, who based two Boeing 737s at Bournemouth. Then, in December, easyJet commenced winter ski flights to Geneva, which have proved popular over the years. Originally Ryanair and Thomson operated to major cities and towns in Europe and the UK. However, they both found it was more profitable to undertake flights to holiday destinations, so their services are now to the Mediterranean holiday resorts. The operations of these low-cost carriers brought about the demise of Palmair, who were no longer able to compete, ceasing operations in October 2010. Presently winter flights will also see Thomson Boeing 767s and 787s flying to the West Indies to connect with P&O Cruises ships. As part of Manchester Airports Group's £45 million investment in Bournemouth, a new terminal was finally built and brought into use in June 2010. Capable of handling 3 million passengers a year, with ten aircraft stands, it opened at a time of worldwide traffic decline. However, passenger numbers slowly increased to 700,000 and the terminal is ready to handle growth over the next few years. Currently, passengers' favoured destination is Palma, followed by Malaga and Alicante. Manchester Airports Group remains upbeat for future business, with Bournemouth being 'a key gateway to Southern England'.

An aerial view of RAF Hurn in the summer of 1944. The recent extensions of the runways to the east and north clearly show up, along with the large number of aircraft dispersals to the north. Aircraft parked include Horsas, Mosquitoes and Typhoons.

A visiting Spitfire of the Battle of Britain Memorial Flight with a Tornado GR4 passing by in the background. This was during one of the annual Seafront Air Festivals.

This Wellington I was modified by the TFU to house a rotating radar aerial above its fuselage. This would enable enemy aircraft and U-boats to be detected, which was something that ground radar could not do. As such it was a forerunner of today's Boeing E-3 Sentry.

Whitleys served with Army Co-operation Command in training airborne forces. As well as parachute training, much time was taken in towing Horsa assault gliders that were to carry troops during the planned invasion.

Having proved unsuitable for its intended role as a bomber, the Armstrong Whitworth Albemarle served as a Horsa glider tug with Nos 295, 296 and 570 Squadrons at Hurn during 1943/44. This was part of the preparations for D-Day on 6 June 1944.

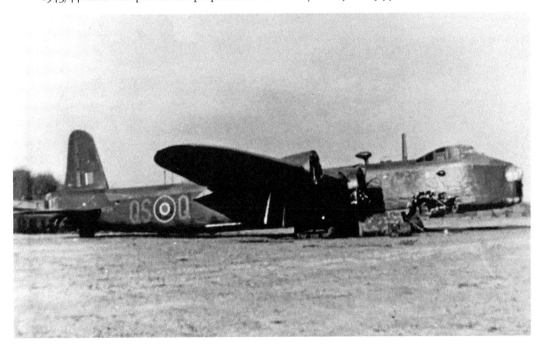

A bomber in trouble – a Short Stirling IV of No. 620 Squadron after a crash landing following flak damage over France in early 1944. The engines have already been removed prior to dismantling the aircraft for removed by 'Queen Mary' low-loaders.

Wing Commander R. Davidson of No. 124 Wing alongside his personal Typhoon in May 1944 – note the code letters 'RD' on the aircraft. Of almost equal interest is the Bournemouth-registered Norton motorcycle – perhaps part of the airfield's motor pool?

Present-day RAF Typhoon FGR4 of No. 29 (Reserve) Squadron visiting the airport in the summer of 2015. Its special markings commemorate a No. 249 Squadron Hurricane whose pilot was awarded a VC while serving in the Battle of Britain during the summer of 1940.

Just after D-Day, ground crews are rearming a Typhoon with underwing rocket projectiles. They were mainly used to attack German road convoys heading towards the invasion area. This Hurn-based Typhoon is at one of the landing grounds established in Normandy.

RAF Typhoon FGR4s of No. 29 Squadron on display at the airport in August 2016. At the time, No. 29 Squadron provided the aircraft for the RAF's Typhoon Display Team.

One of six Northrop P-61 Black Widow night fighters based at the airfield in July 1944. This was the type's first use in Europe and their crews built up operational experience in conjunction with the locally based RAF Mosquito night fighters.

As with the majority of USAAF aircraft, their crews liked to name their aircraft. Here, the smiling crew of P-61 *Shoo-Shoo-Baby* are no exception.

Parked on the north-east side of the airfield are USAAF P-61 night fighters of the 422nd Night Fighter Squadron and RAF Mosquitoes of No. 604 Squadron. The P-61s also undertook trials with the Mosquitoes to see which type of night fighter the Americans considered best.

A modern-day American fighter – a General Dynamics F-16A Falcon of the Dutch Air Force – at Bournemouth in a special colour scheme, preparing for its display at the 2010 Air Festival.

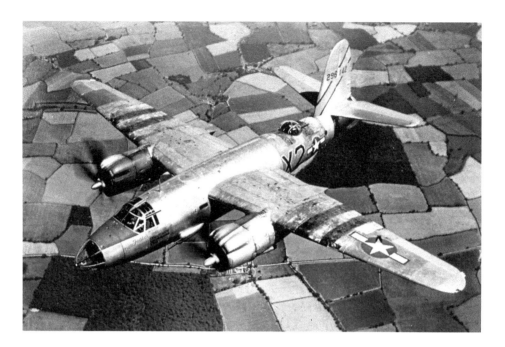

With the departure of the RAF Typhoons, four squadrons of USAAF Marauders of the 397th Bomb Group arrived at Hurn in August 1944. The majority were silver coloured – a contrast to the drab camouflaged RAF Mosquitoes and Typhoons previously operated from Hurn.

There were four B-26 Marauder squadrons within the Bomb Group. A crew from the 599th Bomb Squadron is seen at rest between sorties.

The crew of *Bar Fly* pose in front of their Marauder, which shows thirty-five bombing missions. While at Hurn, the 397th Bomb Group undertook its hundredth bombing mission of the war. The Group moved to Normandy at the end of August 1944.

A reminder of American bombing operations from Hurn was provided by this B-25 Mitchell which appeared at the 2016 Air Festival. The markings are of the Dutch East Indies Air Force.

Lancaster bombers were seen occasionally at Hurn during the war. Nowadays the Battle of Britain Memorial Flight's Lancaster is a frequent visitor to the airport for local shows.

BOAC commenced operations from Hurn at the beginning of 1942. Early in 1944 its Development Flight operated a modified Lancaster especially for trials of the latest version of the Merlin engine. It was later repainted silver and one trial flight took it to California.

*Above and below*: BOAC commenced services to Sydney in May 1945 with converted Lancaster bombers known as Lancastrians. The gun turrets were faired over and the bomb bay removed. Initially only nine passengers, or six sleepers, were carried, space being required for mail.

**MOMENTS IN TIME**

1944    1945    1946    ENG

## THE UK'S FIRST INTERCONTINENTAL AIRPORT

In November 1944, RAF Hurn was transferred to the Ministry of Civil Aviation and became the UK's only intercontinental airport until Heathrow opened two years later.

During that time all the major airlines operated services from Hurn including American Airlines, BOAC, KLM, Pan American, Qantas, Sabena and South African Airlines.

They provided a truly international range of destinations such as Accra, Cairo, Calcutta, Johannesburg, New York, Sydney and Washington.

A flight to Johannesburg could take up to five days, whilst the actual flying time for a journey to Sydney, Australia in a Lancastrian aircraft (a converted Lancaster bomber) took 67¼ hours!

An American Airlines Douglas DC-4 operated the first post-war transatlantic scheduled landplane service from New York into Bournemouth on 24 October 1945. The airline's timetable showed the destination as London (Hurn), not Bournemouth Airport.

The New York service updated; a British Airways Boeing 777 on a Bath Travel charter to New York in July 2004. These charters were operated for a number of years, usually in December for Christmas shopping in 'The Big Apple'.

BOACs initial post-war airliner was the Avro York, which used the wings, engines and tail of the Lancaster bomber, married to a new fuselage. Freight and mail were carried in the forward section of the cabin, with passengers to the rear.

*Above and below*: Meanwhile, Pan American World also operated modern-looking Douglas DC-4s on their North Atlantic services into Bournemouth during 1945, with Constellations from early 1946. As well as New York, there were services from Chicago, Philadelphia and Washington.

A 1948 view of Bournemouth Airport looking west. The terminal area is to the left; the BOAC hangars are top right, where a number of Lancastrians and Yorks are parked. In the foreground are the leftover aircraft hardstandings built for wartime operations.

A diversion from London Heathrow in 1954 due to smog – a common occurrence in the early 1950s. A BOAC Hermes receives an engine change, flanked by an Argonaut to the right, with Constellations and a Stratocruiser in the background.

Diversion from London Gatwick, 2016 style. Lined up in front of the terminal are Airbus A319s of British Airways plus one from easyJet. Diversions are less frequent than in the 1950s and 1960s due to the lack of facilities to handle large numbers of passengers.

Vickers-Armstrongs set up a flight test base at Hurn in 1951. Although first flown from Wisley, the prototype Vickers Valiant bomber undertook its early flying from Hurn. On 12 January 1952 it suffered an uncontrollable engine fire and crashed in the New Forest.

The Valiant prototype parked outside Hangar 106, which Vickers-Armstrongs had taken over from BOAC in 1951. Vickers always referred to the base as its Hurn Site.

The Vickers Varsity prototypes also undertook test flying from Hurn during 1951. Vickers then decided to set up a production line at Hurn, with the first Varsitys delivered to the RAF at the beginning of 1952.

The first Hurn-produced Varsity trainer undertakes engine runs prior to its maiden flight. The majority of Varsities were built at Hurn, the final one being in December 1953. The type served the RAF in a wide range of training roles.

Due to a lack of production space at their Weybridge factory, Vickers-Armstrongs set up a second Viscount production line at Hurn in 1953. The tail of a BEA aircraft is to the left, with an Aer Lingus one awaiting painting. The final Varsity can be seen in the background.

A visit by the Duke of Edinburgh to the Hurn Site in April 1958, with Sir George Edwards – Vickers' Managing Director – following him down the Viscount's steps.

A breakthrough into the North American market came with an order for Viscounts from Trans-Canada Air Lines in November 1952. It was followed by another large order in June 1954 by Capital Airlines of Washington.

The final Viscount to appear at Bournemouth operated £59 enthusiasts' farewell flights on 30 November 1997. This view from the steps shows the terminal buildings in the background.

The School of Air Traffic Control was established at Bournemouth in 1948, using wartime wooden buildings situated near the airport's main entrance. The first students' course was run the following spring.

Area control training underway in the early days. As can be seen, conditions in the huts were rather cramped at the time.

The rather dilapidated wooden buildings used by the school can be seen in this early 1950s group picture of students having just completed their course.

The brand-new school building that was brought into use in the summer of 1962, proving a great step forward for training. It was highly visible from some distance as the outside cladding was bright yellow.

*Above and below*: The school was renamed the College of Air Traffic Control in 1968. As can be seen in this 1974 view of the Operations Room, the new building provided a much more spacious environment for training students.

In the 1970s, the College was tasked with developing radar stations for the forthcoming new control centres at Prestwick and Manchester. This is the trials unit at Bournemouth.

The Bristol Britannia turboprop was liked by crew and passengers. It entered BOAC service in 1957 but was soon outdated by jet airliners such as the Boeing 707 and Douglas DC-8. Two Britannias were normally based at Bournemouth for crew training.

In the early 1950s, de Havilland took over Hangar 102 on the north side of the airport. It was used as the flight test hangar for aircraft produced at their nearby Christchurch factory, which had no hard runway. Vampires and Sea Venoms can be seen parked outside.

Having been built at Christchurch, an early production Vampire trainer is seen on a test flight at Bournemouth at the end of 1952, prior to delivery to the RAF. It has the original-style cockpit canopy with heavy metal framing.

A Sea Venom on test from Bournemouth in 1956, seen overflying Poole Park. Large numbers of Christchurch-built Venoms and Sea Venoms were flight tested from Bournemouth.

The first production Sea Vixen FAW1 on a test flight from Bournemouth in the spring of 1957. The pilot has positioned the fighter over the wartime Holmsley South airfield.

An early Sea Vixen FAW1 on engine runs outside Hangar 102. All aircraft made their first flight from the short runway at Christchurch before landing at Bournemouth for testing.

Seen in company with a preserved Gnat in 2009, preserved XP924 is in its former 899 NAS colours. In September 2014 it was donated to the Fly Navy Heritage Trust at RNAS Yeovilton. At the time, both aircraft were based at Bournemouth with DS Aviation.

Early airline services from Bournemouth were usually provided by Dragon Rapides. Jersey Airlines commenced regular services in 1952.

Pleasure flights at Bournemouth were undertaken by Miles Aerovans in the early 1950s. The wartime control tower is in background, with the fire station huts to its right.

Jersey Airlines replaced their Dragon Rapides with Herons in 1954. This is the prototype Heron, which was fitted with a fixed undercarriage like the first few production aircraft.

During August 1956, BOAC's two Bournemouth-based Britannias were chartered to fly troops to Cyprus during the Suez Crisis. On boarding the airliner they had to remove their boots so as not to damage the newly fitted carpets. Note the Pathé News film crew to the left.

Passengers boarding a British United Viscount in October 1964 for a holiday flight to the Costa Blanca. Note how the style of dress has changed over fifty years and the lack of security.

With the introduction of regular car ferry services in the spring of 1959, the wartime terminal buildings proved inadequate. As a result, this wooden building was moved from Blackbushe to provide additional accommodation.

A view of the facilities inside the 'new' terminal building.

In the 1960s the public were welcomed at the airport. The viewing area outside the restaurant proved a popular location for watching the comings and goings of airliners and people. At the time the airport was known as Bournemouth-Hurn Airport.

With increasing passenger numbers, further wooden extensions to the wartime buildings were added, although many passengers still had to walk a long way to their aircraft.

A de Havilland Mosquito T3 visiting in 1953, landing on the south–north Runway 35. Note the aircraft spotters sitting on the grass alongside the road – a location well known to the author.

In 1956, three former Royal Navy Mosquito 16s were overhauled for the Israeli Air Force. Bearing in mind present-day politics, the event passed unnoticed by the media.

Five Canadian-registered ex-RAF Mosquito B35s arrived in 1957, but progressed no further westwards. Three were scrapped and two ended up on the fire dump.

Refuelling a Hawker Sea Fury FB11 of the Airwork Fleet Requirement Unit. Although obsolete, the fighter proved ideal for the FRU's needs.

The FRU used Fairey Fireflies as target tugs during 1957/58. Note the winch under the forward fuselage, which let out the target on a long cable. After a short time the Fireflies were replaced by Meteor TT20s.

Another of the FRU's Sea Furies outside the hangars in 1958. They remained in service until May 1962, which was well past their anticipated out of service date.

Fifty years later, Bournemouth housed a privately owned Sea Fury. The markings seen on the left-hand side are of the Dutch Navy – the right side was Royal Australian Navy.

A line-up of early Sea Hawk F1s of the Airwork FRU. Those on the left are in normal naval camouflage, whereas the remainder are in a black scheme unique to the FRU. It was to make them more visible as 'targets' while in flight.

Airwork personnel undertake pre-flight maintenance on one of the Sea Hawks. It carries the overall black colour scheme that aided its aerial visual recognition.

Supermarine Scimitar F1s replaced the Sea Hawks from 1966. However, the large twin-engined fighter proved problematical in FRU use and did not remain in service very long.

A gathering of Scimitars outside the Airwork Services hangar, which was situated at the western end of the airport. In the background are the BAC hangars.

The Scimitars were replaced by Hawker Hunter GA11s from 1969. They proved easier to maintain as they were still in current service with the RAF and RN.

In 1969, English Electric Canberra TT18s arrived at Bournemouth to replace the FRU's ageing Meteor target tugs.

A Vickers FB5 Gunbus replica on display at the BAC Families Day in July 1966. Below, a visiting Robinson Redwing undertakes some crazy flying at the same Families Day.

Miles Marathons were used by Derby Airways for a short while in the late 1950s on their services from Derby to the Channel Islands.

A Dan-Air Airspeed Ambassador on an Inclusive Tour holiday flight in the early 1960s. They operated services to Basle and, for Palmair, Majorca.

Car parking, 1960s style. This overflow car park was situated on the grass between the terminal buildings and the School of ATC.

Derby Airways Douglas Dakotas also cleared customs on their services from Derby to the Channel Islands. No problem in those days about parking close to the public enclosure.

Looking in the other direction, Dakotas were introduced by Jersey Airlines for the summer of 1959, pending the introduction of Dart-Heralds. Although difficult to envisage, it is parked in a similar location to that used by present-day Boeing 737s.

Dan-Air again. This time one of their de Havilland Comet 4s is being refuelled and serviced prior to a Corfu IT holiday flight on behalf of Palmair.

The unique Canadair/Conroy CL-44 Guppy was used in October 1970 to carry parts of a damaged One-Eleven. They were being returned to the BAC factory for incorporation into a rebuilt aircraft, which was later delivered to Dan-Air.

Awaiting its fate – the same Guppy in the winter of 2014. Engineers later refitted its engines and there was hope that the Guppy would depart by air, but this was not to be and it ended up in 2017 probably awaiting the scrapman.

Due to the fact that they were produced on the nearby Isle of Wight, Bournemouth has always seen a number of Britten-Norman Islanders. These two are clearing customs in July 1972 prior to a long delivery flight across the Atlantic to Brazil.

Still visiting Bournemouth forty years later, this Turbo-Islander was in use by Britten-Norman as a company run-about/demonstrator.

This Viscount came to grief on 28 January 1972 as the result of a heavy landing. Luckily there were no passengers on board, only the crew, who were rather shaken.

Avro Ansons of all marks visited over the years, usually on communications flights but sometimes providing Air Experience flights to local Air Cadets.

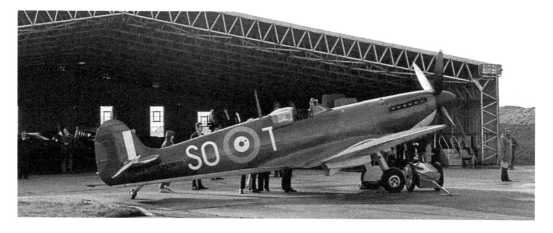

A BoBMF Spitfire visiting in November 1969, parked outside Hangar 268 close to the terminal. Note, to the right of the hangar, the grass mound provided during the war as protection for the hangar against possible bomb blasts.

In October 1970, six Army Beavers called at Bournemouth as the last stage of their twenty-two-day flight home from Singapore to Middle Wallop.

A visiting Westland Whirlwind HAS7 helicopter from RNAS Yeovilton in 1966. Military helicopters were infrequent visitors during the 1960s and 1970s. However, recent years have seen a great many training flights, mainly from Odiham and Yeovilton.

A privately operated Westland Wasp HAS1 visiting the Aviation Museum in 2016.

As well as airliners, various smaller aircraft received overhauls at Bournemouth during the 1960s. Above is a de Havilland Dragon Rapide of the Army Parachute Association and below a de Havilland Chipmunk visiting from Belgium.

The prototype BAC One-Eleven emerges from what was still known as the Vickers-Armstrongs hangar 106 in June 1963. It first flew on the evening of 20 August. Originally built for the RAF, then used by BOAC, extended by Vickers-Armstrongs for Viscount production, below is the rather deserted looking BAC One-Eleven production site.

A special ceremony in progress, marking the handover of the first One-Eleven to Mohawk Airlines of New York in March 1965. The hangar now shows British Aircraft Corporation ownership.

Farewell in May 1984 from the remaining BAC staff to the final Hurn-built One-Eleven.

BAC's Hurn site produced major sections of Concorde noses, which were then transported to Weybridge for incorporation in the forward fuselages under construction there.

The final One-Eleven to visit Bournemouth in October 2009 was one from the Royal Air Force of Oman, whose aircraft had been regular visitors to the airport since 1975.

A link to the days when they were built at the airport, the Aviation Museum has the front fuselage section of a former ETPS One-Eleven aircraft, pointing in the direction of the factory where it was built in July 1973.

The Channel Islands cargo services were taken over by Handley Page Dart Heralds in January 1978; one of the Channel Express fleet is seen off the Hampshire coast. They continued in service until April 1999.

From December 1989 Lockheed Electras joined Channel Express' fleet, sometimes being used on the Channel Islands route, but mainly on the airline's continental freight services.

A view of the main apron and passenger terminal area. The control tower and fire station are to the left, the terminal is to the right and the cargo hangar in the right foreground.

Sud Caravelles were infrequent visitors to Bournemouth. This one from Corse-Air International has flown *Queen Elizabeth 2* passengers across the English Channel from Cherbourg due to a dock strike at Southampton in July 1984.

From the 1970s the Bournemouth Flying Club, originally based in a wartime blister hangar, operated a fleet of Cessnas. This Cessna FA152 is taking part in a local air race.

Bournemouth Flying Club's Aero Commander 114. The personalised registration represents William, John and Marjorie Norris, directors of the club.

Airwork Services' headquarters at the western end of the airport. Over the years the company overhauled civil and military aircraft.

A variety of work in hand in Airwork's Hangar 102. In the foreground is a Sudan Airways Dakota and elsewhere a Marathon, Viking and Dove.

A number of Ghana Air Force Short Skyvans received major overhauls from Airwork Services during 1991. They had arrived by sea via Poole, but returned home by air.

*Above and below*: During their time at Bournemouth, Airwork Services delivered aircraft to many foreign air forces, especially in the Middle East. Here is an Islander en route to the Sultan of Oman AF and a pair of Singapore Air Force BAC Strikemasters stopping off in early 1970.

Basking in the sunshine, this Ilyushin Il-76 had been chartered by Heavy Lift in the spring of 1992 in order to collect equipment for an oil spill exercise.

An Airbus A300ST Beluga specialised freighter arriving in January 2000 to collect a section of an Airbus A300 fuselage from Channel Express.

The main entrance to Bournemouth's 1984 terminal building. In those days it was possible to drop passengers off right outside the entrance doors.

A Bournemouth Flying Club Cessna overflying the terminal area in the late 1980s. A variety of training aircraft are lined up on the apron area.

After chartering aircraft from different airlines for many years, local travel firm Palmair started its own airline operations in April 1993, initially with a BAe 146 'Whisperjet'.

Arranged by Bath Travel and the airport, a British Airways Concorde came to Bournemouth on 'Big Nose Day' in May 1996 to open the airport's main runway extension.

Palmair's Boeing 737 *The Spirit of Peter Bath* returns from another Mediterranean holiday flight in 2009. Underneath it is the former Jet Heritage Hunter 'Gate Guard'.

The Aviation Museum's 737, although a different aircraft, is also named *The Spirit of Peter Bath* – plus seasonal greetings on its nose.

During 1994, Air Atlantique Dakotas undertook a number of nostalgic flights in connection with local D-Day + 50 Anniversary commemorations.

Handley Page Heralds were used on the Channel Island cargo run by a number of airlines. This one belonging to Channel Express has brought tomatoes and flowers into Bournemouth for onward transport by road to major markets.

During the 2000s, the nightly Royal Mail flights were operated by Atlantic Airlines. Their BAe ATP freighters brought mail from the Channel Islands to connect with the Liverpool flight, which was operated by veteran Lockheed Electras. These services ceased at the end of 2015, when all local mail was carried by road.

During the 1980s, Jet Heritage became well known for the restoration of Hawker Hunters. This Hunter F51, a founding member of their fleet, is seen overflying the Needles to the west of the Isle of Wight.

A May 1998 line-up of Hunters overhauled by Jet Heritage. In the foreground is the scarlet-painted flagship, then a Royal Jordanian Air Force fighter, with a Trainer version operated by a syndicate of Cathay Pacific pilots to the rear.

Many of the historic jet fleet seen parked outside the Jet Heritage hangars in 1994.

From 2000, de Havilland Aviation followed Jet Heritage's lead in maintaining historic fighters.

Bournemouth Aviation Museum in 2004, while based on the airport in Hangar 600.

Known to the USAAF as the T-6 Texan and the RAF as the Harvard, the Aviation Museum's example is named *Billie* in honour of its donor.

One of a number of T-6 Texan IIs of the Moroccan Air Force that passed through Bournemouth at the beginning of 2011 on delivery from the US.

The Battle of Britain Memorial Flight has always been a frequent visitor to Bournemouth. Here, their aircraft are seen taking a break while returning home from the Channel Islands.

Two of the airport's handling agent staff are happy to take advantage of a photo opportunity in front of the Lancaster.

A closer view of one of the Flight's Hurricanes after arrival from its Coningsby base to take part in the Bournemouth Seafront Air Festival in August 2011.

Rolls-Royce's Spitfire PR19 being rolled out of a hangar prior to taking part in the 2014 Air Festival. The company considers the Spitfire to be a valuable publicity tool.

The arrival of the Red Arrows. They have brought eleven Hawks – nine for their display plus two spare aircraft. During the 1990s, visits to Bournemouth were arranged by the Bournemouth Red Arrows Association as the Regatta Team was no longer able to fund the visits. From 2008 organisation was taken over by the Bournemouth Air Festival as part of the larger Seafront display.

One of the best positions to view the Red Arrows was the Bournemouth Flying Club cafe, which is unfortunately no longer in business. It was always a good viewpoint to watch the comings and goings at the airport.

The Hawks parked at Bournemouth prior to the 2014 Air Festival. It was the team's fiftieth display season – hence the specially painted tail fins.

During the 1970s and 1980s, a number of popular air shows were held at the airport. Here, a Douglas B-26 Invader displays during the 1980 show.

A McDonnell-Douglas Phantom FGR.2 of No. 111 Squadron taxies in after its display in August 1984 – definitely not a type normally seen at Bournemouth.

FR Aviation's – later Cobham Air Services – fleet of Dassault Falcon 20s carry out electronic warfare exercises with the RAF and Royal Navy. Underwing pods carry an assortment of jammers, chaff dispensers or towed targets.

This Antonov An-124 has arrived with the fuselage of a BAe Nimrod that was to be rebuilt by FR Aviation as a Nimrod MRA4. However, the project was taken back in-house by BAe and was eventually cancelled by the government in October 2010.

Cobham Air Services were part of the FSTA contract to supply Airbus A330 Voyagers to the RAF as dual transport/tankers. Two 'green' airframes were converted at Bournemouth, with the majority being converted by Airbus EADS at Madrid.

The Vulcan to the Sky's preserved Avro Vulcan seeks shelter in the Cobham hangar during the 2010 Air Festival. Normally, the Vulcan did not land at the airport for its display, but operated all the way from its home base at Doncaster Sheffield Airport.

Bournemouth Airport is known for a wide variety of visiting aircraft. Here, a French Army Pilatus PC-6 prepares to return home in May 2014 following a training flight.

Floats are not needed here! A de Havilland Canada Beaver from Norway called while touring the UK during the summer of 2016.

European Aviation operated a fleet of five Boeing 747s for a short while in the early 2000s. They mainly undertook holiday charters from Gatwick and Manchester.

The winter of 1998/99 saw the start of ski holiday flights by British Airways to Chambéry with BAe 146/RJ100s. This RJ100 carries one of the special tail schemes favoured by the airline at the time.

An Embraer 190 of British Airways on short finals to Runway 26. It is arriving to operate a fly/cruise holiday flight to Venice on behalf of Hays Travel.

A Thomson Boeing Dreamliner departs a damp Bournemouth Airport for Barbados and the sun. Regular winter fly/cruise flights carry P&O passengers to their West Indies cruises.

Executive transport in the 1950s and 1960s would probably be by de Havilland Dove. This one was used by Fox's Mints to carry their directors and is seen having cleared customs.

VIP transport, twenty-first century style. This luxury equipped Boeing 747 was used by one of the Sheikhs of Qatar as his preferred transport. Along with a 747SP version, it was maintained at Bournemouth during his visits to the UK.

Royal Air Force of Oman Hercules have been frequent visitors to Bournemouth since the 1980s, collecting a variety of cargo to take back to Oman.

Not all Hercules visitors are military ones. Landing on Runway 08 is an Oil Spill Response Ltd Hercules in connection with an oil pollution exercise held in the Solent.

Other military activity sees both Royal Navy and Army Wildcats at the present time; they visit while crew training from Yeovilton.

Visitors from Boscombe Down include aircraft of Empire Test Pilots School and QinetiQ. This is one of the Empire Test Pilots School's two BAe 146s.

The latest RAF transports also appear at Bournemouth on crew training. They include the Airbus Atlas or Boeing Globemaster, as seen here.

A visiting Belgian Air Force Westland Sea King wearing a special colour scheme to mark its twenty-five years in service. It had stopped off for fuel en route to a Royal Navy air show at Culdrose.

A variety of sizes in helicopter training at Bournemouth. Initial training is currently available in types like this Schweizer 300. At the other end of the scale, RAF Chinooks are frequent visitors from their base at Odiham.

A regular event on the airport's summer calendar is the Dorset Plane Pull, where teams have to pull a 35,000 kg Boeing 737 over a distance of 50 metres. The Plane Pull has raised substantial amounts for local charities over the years.

The RAF version of the Plane Pull – a team from No. 29 Squadron haul one of their Eurofighter Typhoons at the 2015 event.

This view of the Aviation Museum shows its proximity to the airport. Access is encouraged to the majority of aircraft cockpits. Viewing platforms are provided for visitors to have a better view of activity over the fence at the airport.

The Museum's volunteers have recently repainted its Sepecat Jaguar fighter to its original No. 226 OCU colour scheme.

The approach road to Bournemouth International Airport's 1980s terminal. The terminal was adequate for the fifty- or sixty-seat airliners in service at the time.

The new departures terminal opened in June 2010, to be followed by the arrivals terminal, which opened the following October. They were part of Manchester Airports Group's £45 million investment in Bournemouth Airport.

When brought into use in 2011, the energy-efficient arrivals terminal was smaller than originally planned in order to reduce costs.

The 2010 departure terminal just prior to completion. Additional car parking areas are being provided in the background. Below shows a quiet period in in the Departure Terminal.

At the Northern Aviation Business Park, AIM Altitude's large complex, opened in December 2016, combined their various cabin interior furnishing production sites.

Also at the Business Park, Signature TECHNICAir is an authorised service centre for the Citation range of executive jets. Their Hangar 100 also handles visiting executive aircraft.

The extensive Curtiss-Wright complex, which was brought into use at the beginning of 2017.

Current airline services see Tui Boeing 737s, easyJet Airbus A320s and Ryanair 737s.